Count your Blessings

Life is great

Antony Melvin D Paul

BookLeaf Publishing

India | USA | UK

To God, whose grace and love guide me through every step of this journey. Your blessings are the foundation of all that I am and all that I aspire to be.

To my parents, whose unwavering support and endless love have shaped me into the person I am today. Your sacrifices and wisdom are the pillars of my strength.

To my beloved wife, whose love and companionship make every day brighter. You are my rock, my confidant, and my greatest blessing.

To my son, whose laughter and curiosity remind me of the beauty and wonder in the world. You inspire me to be better every day.

To my sisters, whose bond and encouragement have been a constant source of joy and comfort. Your presence in my life is a gift I cherish deeply.

To my friends, whose loyalty and kindness make life's journey so much richer. You remind me of the true meaning of friendship and the blessings it brings.

Thank you all for making life so beautiful and for always reminding me of the countless blessings we have. This book is dedicated to you, with all my love and gratitude.

Acknowledgement

First and foremost, I extend my deepest gratitude to the Lord Almighty, whose grace and blessings have guided me through every step of this journey. Without His divine presence, none of this would have been possible.

To my parents, who have been my pillars of strength and wisdom, thank you for your unwavering belief in me. Your love and sacrifices have shaped me into the person I am today.

To my beloved wife, your endless support and encouragement have been my greatest source of inspiration. Your love is the light that guides me through the darkest of times.

To my son, you are my pride and joy. Your curiosity and zest for life remind me daily of the beauty and wonder in the world.

To my sisters, thank you for your constant love and for always being there for me. Your support means the world to me.

To my friends, your camaraderie and encouragement have been invaluable. Thank you for standing by me through thick and thin.

To my managers, your trust in my abilities and your guidance have been instrumental in my success. Your belief in me has given me the confidence to pursue my dreams.

Each of you has played a crucial role in my journey, and I am profoundly grateful for your love, support, and faith in me. This book is a testament to the blessings I count every day, and I dedicate it to all of you who have made this possible.

Preface

In the hustle and bustle of our daily lives, it's easy to overlook the simple joys and blessings that surround us. This collection of poems, "Count Your Blessings: Life is Great," is a heartfelt reminder to pause, reflect, and appreciate the myriad of gifts that life offers us each day.

Through these verses, we journey through moments of gratitude, love, and wonder. Each poem is a celebration of the beauty found in the ordinary and the extraordinary, encouraging us to embrace a mindset of thankfulness. Whether it's the warmth of the sun on our skin, the laughter shared with loved ones, or the quiet strength found in solitude, these poems highlight the countless reasons we have to be grateful.

As you turn these pages, may you find inspiration to cherish the present, recognize the blessings in your life, and cultivate a heart full of gratitude. Life, with all its ups and downs, is a precious gift. Let these poems serve as a gentle nudge to count your blessings and remember that, indeed, life is great.

Righteousness in the Riots

Amok in the night in a bus to leave,
began a riot, the heart of chaos,
when stones flying, fires burning, people
screaming, buses on fire, the cries of despair
and fear,
dark shadows loomed large,
A mother's love shines through the gloom.

Amidst the riots, fierce and wild, She stands
her ground to save her child.
With courage fierce and heart so pure,
She faces danger, strong and sure.
Her arms a shield, her voice a prayer,
Protecting him with tender care.
Through fire and fear, she does not sway,
Her love the light to guide the way.

For in her heart, a sacred vow,
To keep him safe, no matter how.
Oh, blessed son, with mother dear,
Her sacrifice wipes away your fear.

Her love, a beacon, ever bright,
Guides you through the darkest night.
In gratitude, you bow your head.

For all the tears and blood she shed.
Her strength, her grace, her endless care,
A gift beyond compare.
Now grown and strong, you stand with pride,
Her lessons deep within you guide.
With every step, you honor her,

The mother who made life a blur.
For all she's done, for all she's been,
Her love, a force unseen.

You dedicate your life to show,
The depth of love she'll always know.
A mother's sacrifice, a son's embrace,
Together, they find their place.
In love and honor, hand in hand,
A bond unbroken, forever grand.

Count your blessing,
For many motherless,
For when we have parents, celebrate them,
For blessings come, as mothers too.

A Middle Class Blessing

In a home where love is the guiding light,
We grew up strong, with hearts so bright.
Though middle class, our wealth was clear, In
the bonds of family, ever near.

With simple means, we learned to share,
In every moment, love and care.
Our parents' wisdom, gentle and kind,
Shaped our hearts and minds.

No riches grand, no lavish ways,
But joy and laughter filled our days.
In every meal, a feast of love,
Blessings sent from up above.

We learned the value of hard work,
In every task, we did not shirk.
With dreams held high and spirits free,
We faced the world, our destiny.

Through every trial, hand in hand,
Together strong, we made our stand.
In every hug, in every smile,
We found our strength, mile by mile.

A family bound by ties so true,
In every storm, we made it through.
With hearts so full, we understand,
The greatest wealth is close at hand.

For in our home, with love so pure,
We found a life that would endure.
A middle class, yet richly blessed,
In family love, we found our rest.

The Lord's Abundant Care

In every step, through joy and strife,
The Lord has guided all our life.
From humble starts, with little means,
To blessings rich, beyond our dreams.

With slippers worn on dusty roads,
To cars that lighten heavy loads.
From clothes once new, just once a year,
To choices now, both far and near.

In every moment, big and small,
The Lord has watched and cared for all.
His hand has led us through the night,
To brighter days and clearer sight.

With every gift, our hearts expand,
In gratitude, we understand.
The blessings flow, both great and small,
A testament to His love for all.

Through trials faced and mountains climbed,
His grace has been our constant rhyme.
From simple joys to grander things,
The Lord's provision always brings.

In every tear, in every smile,
He's walked with us through every mile.
From humble homes to dreams fulfilled,
His love and care have always willed.

So let us count each blessing true,
With hearts of thanks in all we do.
For every step, His love imparts,
The Lord's abundant care and heart.

From Struggles to Success

A little boy, with dreams so bright,
Struggled hard, both day and night.
With English words, he fought to speak,
Made fun of, called small and weak.

Each letter seemed a mountain high,
Spelling words, he'd often sigh.
But deep within, a fire burned,
A mission clear, a lesson learned.

He put in yards, with heart and soul,
Determined to achieve his goal.
From every stumble, every fall,
He rose again, standing tall.

With every book, with every page,
He honed his craft, he set the stage.
From knowing nothing, he grew wise,
A journey seen through tear-filled eyes.

Today, he writes with passion true,
In newspapers, journals, poems too.
His words now flow, a river wide,
A testament to the boy inside.

The blessing of his journey long,
From silent tears to victory's song.
A story of resilience bright,
A beacon in the darkest night.

For every child who feels the same,
His story lights a hopeful flame.
From struggles deep, success can rise,
A dream fulfilled before our eyes.

Angels of Love

When shadows fall and hope seems lost,
When life's harsh winds leave us tossed,
In moments dark, when hearts are sore,
Love steps in, to heal and more.

Down and out, feeling misunderstood,
Unseen, unsupported, as no one should.
In silence deep, a whisper sweet, Love arrives,
our souls to greet.
Like angels sent from realms above,
People come, with hearts of love.

They lift us up, they hold us near,
Their presence wipes away our fear.
In eyes that see beyond our pain,
In hands that help us rise again,
Their kindness shines, a guiding light,
Turning darkness into bright.

With every word, with every touch,
They show us that we matter much.
In love's embrace, we find our way,
Through night to dawn, to a brighter day.

For when we're down, and all seems bleak,
It's love that finds us, strong yet meek.
In friends and strangers, angels true,
God's love shines through, in all they do.

So, cherish those who come our way,
Their love a blessing, come what may.
For in their hearts, we find our peace,
And in their care, our worries cease.

A Dedication to Mentors and Managers

In the journey of our striving,
Through the paths of dreams arriving,
Mentors and managers, blessings true,
Lift our talents, guide us through.

With wisdom shared and promises kept,
In their support, our fears are swept.
They see the spark within our eyes,
And help us reach for higher skies.

Their faith in us, a guiding light,
Through darkest days and longest night.
They give us platforms, let us shine,
Their only goal, our success divine.
With every word of kind advice,
They help us grow; they help us rise.

Their care and love, a precious gift,
In their belief, our spirits lift.
Though words can never quite repay,
The debt of gratitude we say,

This poem stands, a humble token,
For all the love and care unspoken.
To mentors, managers, hearts so true,
This dedication is for you.
Your affection, concern, and endless grace,
Are blessings time cannot erase.

Thank you for the paths you've paved,
For every talent you have saved.
In your support, we find our way,
And for your kindness, we humbly pray.

Unsung Heroes

In moments when we're lost and weak,
When shadows fall and futures bleak,
House help, doctors, nurses too,
Support staff, blessings through and through.

With hands that heal and hearts that care,
They lift us up from dark despair.
Their dedication, pure and true,
A guiding light in all we do.

House help, with their tireless grace,
Keep our homes a loving place.
Their work, though often left unseen,
Is vital to our daily scene.

Good doctors, with their healing hands,
Stand by us, through life's demands.
Their knowledge, skill, and gentle touch,
In times of need, mean so much.

Nurses, angels by our side,
With endless patience, they provide.
Comfort, care, and tender might,
Through every day and sleepless night.

Support staff, in their quiet way,
Ensure that we are safe each day.
Their efforts, though they may seem small,
Are blessings that uplift us all.

For all they do, for all they give,
In gratitude, our hearts must live.
To them and to their families dear,
We owe a debt of thanks sincere.

So let us honor, let us praise,
These unsung heroes of our days.
With utmost gratitude, we say,
Thank you for your light, your way.

A Penniless Blessing

In pockets bare, no coins to spare,
Yet blessings bloom, beyond compare.
With empty hands, we find the grace,
In simple joys, a warm embrace.

The morning sun, a golden hue,
The sky so vast, a tranquil blue.
A bird's sweet song, the rustling leaves,
In nature's arms, our hearts believe.

No wealth to count, no gold to hold,
But stories shared, and hands to fold.
In laughter's echo, love's pure light,
We find our wealth, in day and night.

No need to chase what others claim,
For in our hearts, we hold the flame.
Of gratitude, and peace of mind,
In every moment, joy we find.

So let us cherish what we see,
The simple gifts, the moments free.
For even without a penny's gleam,
We live our lives, a blessed dream.

The Blessing of a Hug

In moments dark, when spirits fall,
A simple hug can say it all.
When tears flow free, and hearts are sore,
A hug can heal, and so much more.

In times of loss, when words are few,
A hug can bridge the gap to you.
When sadness wraps its cold embrace,
A hug brings warmth, a gentle grace.

When skies are gray, and hope seems thin,
A hug can let the light back in.
In life's low ebb, when strength is gone,
A hug can help us carry on.

So let us share this gift so pure,
A hug can comfort, heal, and cure.
For those who wait, in need of love,
A hug's a blessing from above.

A Blessing called Child

In your arms, a miracle lies,
A tiny soul with endless skies.
A blessing rare, a gift so true,
A child to cherish, through and through.

For many hearts, this dream denied,
Yet in your care, this joy resides.
Treasure every laugh and tear,
Each moment fleeting, precious, dear.

Not just for wealth or worldly gain,
But teach them love, through joy and pain.
Instill in them a heart so kind,
With values strong, and open mind.

Guide them to be a light so bright,
To stand for truth, to fight for right.
With compassion as their guiding star,
They'll change the world, both near and far.

For in their hands, the future lies,
A chance to lift, to heal, to rise.
So, shape them with your love and care,
A blessing to the world, so rare.

A Second Chance

You stood at heaven's open gate,
A brush with fate, a twist so great.
Yet here you are, with heart so strong,
A second chance where you belong.

Your deeds of kindness, pure and true,
The love you gave, it carried you.
Your parents' blessings, whispered prayers,
Their steadfast love, beyond compare.

Your family's warmth, their endless care,
A beacon bright, in darkest air.
Your friends' support, their prayers so deep,
A bond that time and fate can't sweep.

Through trials faced, you found your way,
A miracle, a brand new day.
So let us celebrate this gift,
Your life, your love, your spirit's lift.

For in your heart, a light does shine,
A testament to love divine.
A second chance, a life renewed,
A blessing shared, with gratitude.

A Balcony View

One day I sat, in quiet thought,
Upon my balcony, life I sought.
The world below, in chaos spun,
Yet in that moment, peace begun.

I saw the rush, the endless race,
Yet felt a calm, a gentle grace.
A roof above, a home so warm,
A shelter safe from any storm.

With food each day upon my plate,
A blessing true, I contemplate.
Family near, their love so bright,
Friends who bring such pure delight.

A job to do, a purpose clear,
Good health and strength, year after year.
As I looked out, my heart did see,
So many with less, yet filled with glee.

In simple joys, their hearts content,
No wealth to show, no riches spent.
How can I then, compare, complain,
When others smile through joy and pain?

For in this life, the gifts we hold,
Are not just measured by the gold.
But by the love, the health, the cheer,
The blessings that we hold so dear.

So, as I sat, and watched the day,
I thanked the stars, in my own way.
For all I have, and all I see,
A life of grace, a heart set free.

A Lesson in Gratitude
for the selfish

In life's grand play, some seek to gain,
Yet often miss the joy in rain.
They crave the stars, the moon, the gold,
But fail to see the warmth they hold.

With friends so dear, a gift so rare,
Yet selfish hearts, they do not care.
They put their needs above the rest,
And miss the chance to be their best.

They rant and rave, and always yearn,
For things they think they must discern.
But in their quest, they overlook,
The blessings written in life's book.

For friends who stand through thick and thin,
Are treasures found deep within.
To give, to share, to lend a hand,
Is where true wealth and joy expand.

So let this be a gentle nudge,
To those who in their hearts may judge.
To see the light in what they own,
And cherish love they've always known.

For life is short, and moments fleet,
It's in our hearts that blessings meet.
So open eyes, and hearts so wide,
And let true gratitude be your guide.

Blessed by Mother India

In the heart of India, where cultures blend,
A land of wonders, without end.
Born in this soil, a blessing true,
With lessons rich, and skies so blue.

Humility, our guiding light,
In every heart, a beacon bright.
Generosity, a trait we share,
With open arms, we show we care.

As perfect hosts, we welcome all,
In every home, no guest too small.
To share, to give, to sacrifice,
In love and kindness, we find our spice.

From North to South, and East to West,
In unity, we are truly blessed.
So many cultures, vibrant, grand,
Together strong, we proudly stand.

Let's spend our days in love, not hate,
For in our hearts, we hold our fate.
With heads held high, and hands to build,
A nation's dream, with hope fulfilled.

In every field, let's strive to be,
The best we can, for all to see.
With values strong, and spirits high,
We'll touch the stars, we'll reach the sky.

For India's heart beats in us all,
A legacy that stands so tall.
Let's cherish this, our sacred land,
And build a future, hand in hand.

The Gift of Giving

In the heart of every soul,
Lies a gift that makes us whole.
The habit of giving, pure and true,
A blessing that comes back to you.

Not just in wealth, or coins of gold,
But in the warmth of hands we hold.
In knowledge shared, and wisdom spread,
In lifting hearts, and breaking bread.

To give from what we have each day,
In every small and simple way.
A helping hand, a listening ear,
A gesture kind, to bring us near.

For in the act of giving, we find,
A joy that fills the heart and mind.
It's in our nature, deep and wide,
A part of us we should not hide.

Teach the children, young and bright,
To give with love, to share the light.
For in their hearts, the future lies,
A world of giving, where kindness flies.

Let's make this habit part of our core,
To give and share, and so much more.
For generations yet to come,
A legacy of love, for everyone.

In giving, we create a place,
Where love and hope can find their space.
A world made beautiful and free,
By hearts that give unconditionally.

Live in the moment

In the rush of life, we often stray,
From the beauty of the present day.
We chase the future, dreams untold,
And miss the moments pure as gold.

But here and now, in this brief time,
Lies a treasure, so sublime.
Each breath we take, each sight we see,
A blessing given, wild and free.

The morning sun, the evening's glow,
The gentle breeze, the rivers flow.
In every heartbeat, every smile,
Life's simple joys, make it worthwhile.

So let us pause, and truly see,
The gift of now, for you and me.
Be thankful for each dawn we greet,
For every day is life complete.

Don't dwell on what tomorrow brings,
Or fret about uncertain things.
For in this moment, we are whole,
With grateful hearts and peaceful souls.

Embrace the present, hold it tight,
With love and joy, and pure delight.
For every day we wake anew,
Is a blessing, pure and true.

Life's Blessings, Hidden and Bright

In the quiet moments and the bustling days,
Lie life's blessings, in a myriad of ways.
From the morning sun's gentle, golden embrace,
To the loved one's smile, a tender, familiar face.

Each heartbeat is a gift, each breathe a sigh of grace,
In the tapestry of time, they weave a sacred space.
Where joy and sorrow dance, hand in hand they glide,
For in the depths of darkness, light is magnified.

Adversity, though daunting, is a blessing in disguise,
It nudges us forward, though tears may fill our eyes.

For every storm that rages, every challenge
faced with might,
Shapes us, molds us, turns our wrongs to
right.

The mountains that we climb, the valleys we
descend,
Teach us to persevere, to bend but never end.
For in each trial, there's a lesson, a wisdom to
be found,
In every fall, a rise, as we lift from off the
ground.

The seeds of hope are planted, in soils rich
and deep,
In the fertile fields of struggle, where dreams
begin to leap.
For blessings come in whispers, in shadows,
and in light,
Guiding us through the darkness, to the
dawn's early sight.

So, cherish every moment, every triumph,
every pain,
For life's blessings are abundant, like the
summer's gentle rain.
Embrace the ebb and flow, the highs and
lows, the strife,
For it's through these varied measures, we
truly live our life.

In the symphony of existence, let gratitude be
our song,
For every step, each stumble, makes our
journey strong.
Life's blessings are boundless, both the seen
and the obscure,
In every beat of the heart, the soul finds its
cure.

The Forgotten Treasure

In the garden of life, love blooms bright,
A treasure abundant, bathed in light.
Yet, often overlooked, taken for granted,
Its presence unvalued, its roots unplanted.

When love arrives in vast, overflowing
streams,
It's easy to neglect its precious beams.
For in the comfort of its warm embrace,
We forget to cherish, to hold with grace.

The heart grows blind to love's gentle touch,
Thinking it eternal, never too much.
In the rush of days, it's set aside,
Its worth dismissed; its power denied.

Yet, when the garden wilts, and love is gone,
The heart awakens, cold and forlorn.
Regret seeps in like an endless night,
Realizing the loss of love's pure light.

For love, once abundant, now a faded dream,
Was a blessing unkept, a golden gleam.
In hindsight, we see the folly and pain,
Of undervaluing love, treating it in vain.

We long for the touch that warmed our soul,
For the love that made us whole.
But in our haste, we failed to see,
The true essence of love's decree.

So, let us honor love in its prime,
Cherish its moments, throughout time.
For love, when treasured, grows ever strong,
A timeless melody, a heartfelt song.

In the garden of life, may we always
remember,
To value love's fire, its glowing ember.
For love is a gift, both rare and sweet,
A blessing to hold, and never to defeat.

Blessings in Solitude

In the quiet corners of the night,
When shadows cast their endless flight,
There dwells a solitude so deep,
A silent whisper, a soul to keep.

Loneliness, a companion true,
In the absence of love and comrade crew,
Yet, within its still and solemn space,
Lies a hidden, gentle grace.

Aspiring for love's warm embrace,
For camaraderie's familiar face,
Yet, time and again, hearts left to yearn,
A flame of hope, a steady burn.

Eyes lift to the heavens above,
Seeking solace, seeking love.
And in that celestial, tranquil sky,
A presence felt, a soft reply.

A mother's smile, tender and bright,
A beacon in the darkest night.
Her hand upon your weary shoulder,
Turns the loneliness to a warmth much
bolder.

In that sacred, quiet communion,
Loneliness becomes a blessed union.
For in the solitude, you find,
A peace that soothes the restless mind.

No longer bound by earthly ties,
Your spirit soars, your heart complies.
In her smile, you feel the grace,
Of love that time cannot erase.

So, in the silence, in the calm,
Find the blessing, the healing balm.
For loneliness, though stark and real,
Holds a beauty, a love you feel.

And in those moments, pure and sweet,
Where heaven and earth quietly meet,
You realize you're not alone,
In solitude, a home is shown.

Purpose of Life

In the silk of time, we find our place,
A fleeting moment, a sacred space.
Life, a gift, a blessing so rare,
A chance to breathe, to love, to care.

Seek your purpose, let your heart lead,
In every action, plant a seed.
For dreams are whispers of the soul,
Guiding us towards our ultimate goal.

Embrace each dawn with hope anew,
The path is yours, the journey true.
With courage, rise, and face the fight,
For we have but one chance to get it right.

In kindness, strength, and love, we grow,
Through trials and triumphs, we come to
know,
That life's true purpose, pure and bright,
Is to live with passion and shine our light.

Let us cherish each moment, make it count,
Climb every mountain, scale every mount.
For in this life, our one grand chance,
We find our purpose and join the dance.

The Blessing of Generosity

In a world where we often seek to gain,
There's a virtue that shines through the rain.
A gentle act, a giving heart,
Generosity sets us worlds apart.

More than treasures, more than gold,
It's a story of kindness, humbly told.
To give more than we ever desire,
Lights a spark, ignites a fire.

In the warmth of a helping hand,
We find a joy so pure, so grand.
Blessings multiply, far and wide,
In the hearts where love and giving reside.

For when we give, we truly see,
The profound gift of empathy.
In selfless acts, in open hands,
Lies the grace that understands.

So let us cherish this golden thread,
Of kindness in the lives we've led.
To give, to share, to be the light,
In generosity, we find delight.

Staying Happy Despite the Haters

In a world where hearts might sting,
With words like arrows, sharp as anything,
We'll dance our way through life's parade,
With joy and laughter, never to fade.

For love, they say, can be so sweet,
Yet sometimes bitter folks we meet.
They sneer and snub, they turn away,
But we stay blessed, come what may.

We'll wear our smiles, bright and wide,
With happiness that's hard to hide.
Their despise can't dim our sunny skies,
Our spirits soar, oh how we rise!

For every frown and nasty jest,
We'll count our blessings, we're the best.
With every laugh and cheerful cheer,
We chase away each pesky jeer.

So let them mutter, moan, and stew,
Our hearts are warm, our love is true.
Through life, we'll skip and sing this song,
We're blessed, we're happy, all day long!

The Blessing of Humility

In the garden where virtues grow,
Amidst the tallest trees in row,
There blooms a flower, soft and pure,
Its gentle grace, forever sure.

Humility, a blessing rare,
A tender heart that's kind and fair.
As we rise and stature gain,
Let's nurture this, like gentle rain.

For in the heights where eagles soar,
Humility can offer more.
A grounded soul in lofty skies,
Brings wisdom, light, to all who rise.

With every step we proudly take,
Let's wear humility, never fake.
For true greatness lies within,
In humble hearts that always win.

So as we climb life's mighty tower,
Let's cherish this, our greatest power.
In all we do, in all we see,
Let humility be our key.